EDGE
BOOKS™

THE WORLD OF ARTIFICIAL INTELLIGENCE

ARTIFICIAL INTELLIGENCE
AND ENTERTAINMENT

AN AUGMENTED READING EXPERIENCE

BY TAMMY ENZ

CONSULTANT:
David S. Touretzky
Research Professor
of Computer Science
Carnegie Mellon University
Pittsburgh, Pennsylvania

CAPSTONE PRESS
a capstone imprint

Edge Books are published by Capstone Press
1710 Roe Crest Drive,
North Mankato, Minnesota 56003
www.mycapstone.com

Library of Congress Cataloging-in-Publication Data is available on the Library of Congress website:
978-1-5435-5472-4 (library binding)
978-1-5435-5476-2 (eBook PDF)

Summary: Discusses the ways artificial intelligence is used in various areas of the entertainment industry.

Editorial Credits
Karen Aleo and Christopher Harbo, editors; Brann Garvey, designer; Pam Mitsakos and Tracy Cummins, media researchers; Kathy McColley, production specialist

Image Credits
Alamy: age fotostock, 22-23; AP Photo: Seth Wenig, 10; Getty Images: Anadolu Agency/Salih Zeki Fazlioglu, 26-27 (top), Bloomberg/Yuriko Nakao, 25, Yvonne Hemsey, 7; iStockphoto: mphillips007, 20-21; Newscom/MCT/ Handout, 16-17, YNA/Yonhap News, 12-13 (top); Shutterstock: Action Sports Photography, 24, Andrey Suslov, 28-29, Brian Kienzle, 12 (bottom left), EpicStockMedia, 26 (bottom middle), ESB Professional, 14-15, ImageFlo, 4-5, khoamartin, 19, Mark Nazh, Cover, MS711, 18, Supphachai Salaeman, Design Element; The Image Works: ©dpa/ullstein bild, 8-9

Printed and bound in the USA.   PA48

1 Ask an adult to download the app.

Capstone 4D
Education

2 Scan any page with the star.

3 Enjoy your cool stuff!

— OR —

Use this password at capstone4D.com

entertain.54724

CONTENTS

AI AND ENTERTAINMENT

You are standing in your bedroom, but you're in the middle of a war zone. Laser beams fly over your head. Explosions spew dirt into the air. Suddenly your favorite video game character pops out from under the bed. You try to dodge its blasts, but the character guesses your move. Game over!

You pull off your **augmented reality** (AR) glasses and flop down on your bed. A robot rolls up next to you. It knows you're sad because you lost the game. It starts playing your favorite song to cheer you up. It then snaps a photo of your frowny-face, which makes you laugh.

Does this scene sound like it's from a futuristic movie or TV show? It's not. This reality is closer than you think. The world of entertainment is already changing because of artificial intelligence (AI)—and it's about to explode!

augmented reality—a computer-generated world created over the real world

CHAPTER 1

EARLY AI

Artificial intelligence is the ability of machines to solve problems and perform tasks that would normally require human intelligence. One part of AI is known as **machine learning**. A machine learns by taking in large amounts of data and analyzing it. Then it **predicts** what will happen next based on the information it received. The more information AI analyzes, the better the machine's predictions become.

DEEP BLUE

Many people first saw AI in action in 1997. Millions watched a six-game chess match. One player was the world chess champion, Garry Kasparov. The other was a supercomputer called Deep Blue created by the International Business Machines Corporation (IBM).

machine learning—the way a computer learns

predict—to say what you think will happen in the future

03

IBM's Deep Blue towers over a computer monitor that shows the supercomputer's chess moves.

World chess champion Garry Kasparov squares off against Deep Blue during their first matchup in 1996.

This was not the first match between Kasparov and Deep Blue. They had squared off one year earlier. Kasparov won that match four games to two. But now Deep Blue had received many upgrades and its engineers were hungry for a rematch.

The 1997 rematch started well for Kasparov. He won the first game. But Deep Blue came back with a win in game two. Then the next three games ended in a tie. Kasparov really began feeling the pressure going into game six. In less than 20 moves, he lost the final game, and the match, to the computer program. Deep Blue had used AI to out-think a human.

How did Deep Blue pull off the win? Chess experts helped program its **software**. They gave Deep Blue the coding for different chess moves. With this data, Deep Blue used **strategy** and **logic** to win the game.

FACT

Deep Blue could analyze more than 200 million possible chess positions per second.

software—programs used by a computer

strategy—a plan for winning a game or contest

logic—careful and correct reasoning and thinking

WATSON PLAYS *JEOPARDY*

In the years following Deep Blue's win, computers became even more advanced. They could process huge amounts of data very quickly. By the mid-2000s, computer engineers at IBM were ready to test AI in a different game. They set their sights on *Jeopardy*.

Former champion Ken Jennings prepares to face IBM's Watson on *Jeopardy* in 2011.

Jeopardy is a TV **trivia** game show in which players must understand language. Players are first given an answer, and then they must provide the question that goes with it. For instance, a player might be given this answer: "He lost his chess match to Deep Blue in 1997." Then the player must provide the question: "Who is Garry Kasparov?"

For a machine to play *Jeopardy*, it would need to learn a lot of trivia. It would also need to understand phrases. And it would need to work backward from an answer to create the question.

DOCTOR WATSON

After *Jeopardy*, IBM continued to improve Watson and shrink its size. Now the supercomputer is helping doctors plan cancer treatments. It **scans** through medical journals. It looks at thousands of cases and studies a patient's needs. Then it comes up with a treatment plan. Soon Watson will help treat other diseases too.

To tackle these AI challenges, IBM created Watson. This supercomputer took years to design and was the size of a large bedroom. To prepare for *Jeopardy*, engineers programmed it with 200 million pages of information. Then it challenged two of *Jeopardy*'s most successful champions in 2011. The competition was fierce, but in the end Watson easily beat both humans.

trivia—small details or little-known facts

scan—to look at closely and carefully

SELF-TAUGHT ALPHAGO

A company called DeepMind soon followed Watson's success. DeepMind's goal is to use machine learning to solve problems. In 2014 it began work on AlphaGo. This computer program used AI to learn the ancient board game Go.

Go is played on a square grid with black and white stones. The goal is to try to surround and capture an **opponent's** stones. The game's rules are simple. But the possible moves are endless—which makes the game very difficult for a machine to learn. But DeepMind faced the challenge. It showed AlphaGo thousands of human Go matches to understand the game. It also had AlphaGo play the game against different copies of itself to become a better player. DeepMind's efforts paid off. In March 2016, AlphaGo beat master Go player Lee Sedol four games to one.

After AlphaGo's success, DeepMind took machine learning to the next level with AlphaGo Zero. This **enhanced** AI program didn't need to watch human Go matches at all. AlphaGo Zero learned by just playing Go against itself. In 2017 AlphaGo Zero beat the original AlphaGo 100 games to none!

FACT

AlphaGo Zero was not programmed specifically for Go. It can be used to help solve problems in many areas. For example, it can help develop new medicines.

Go master Lee Sedol makes a move against AlphaGo in a 2016 match.

opponent—a person who competes against another person

enhanced—made better or greater

CHAPTER 2

AI IN VIDEO GAMES

You may not have played against AlphaGo or Watson, but you've likely seen artificial intelligence in video games. Many video games use AI to learn your style of play. AI allows the game's characters to adjust to your actions. For example, over time AI learns your combat patterns, or how you fight. Then it creates enemies that can predict your moves. The better AI becomes at predicting your actions, the more challenging the game becomes.

But would human players stand a chance against a full AI-run game? Because AI can think and react faster than humans, it can easily win. In real-time games like *WarCraft*, game designers had to simplify AI to improve a player's odds. Many designers want to limit the role of AI in video games so people still have a chance to win.

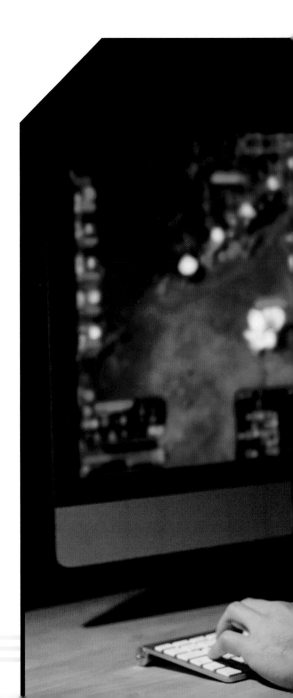

AI makes video games more unpredictable and challenging to defeat.

digital—involving or relating to the use of computers

CREATING VIDEO GAMES

AI isn't just important to playing video games. It also plays a big part in creating the games in the first place. For instance, AI helps programmers make game characters behave more realistically. Instead of pre-programming movements, characters respond to what is going on around them.

Artificial intelligence is also used to help game designers do their jobs. The developers of the 2011 game *The Elder Scrolls V: Skyrim* used AI to create simple quests. And 2016's *No Man's Sky* used AI to create a huge game world with lifelike creatures no one had ever seen before.

AI may one day even create all new games from scratch. Researcher Michael Cook's Angelina program thinks up games that no one has thought of before. It finds images on the Internet and uses them to create interesting backgrounds. Angelina also uses social media and news stories to come up with game ideas. It then develops rules to go along with them.

The Elder Scrolls V: Skyrim also used AI to allow non-player characters to behave based on what was happening around them.

AUGMENTED REALITY AND VIRTUAL REALITY GAMES

Artificial intelligence is a must in creating augmented reality (AR) and **virtual reality** (VR) games. AR games blend the digital world with the real world. People use special glasses or other digital devices to see the game come alive in a real space. Characters can bounce across the floor and do other things in the room. For example, *Minecraft* characters might jump up on a coffee table in your home.

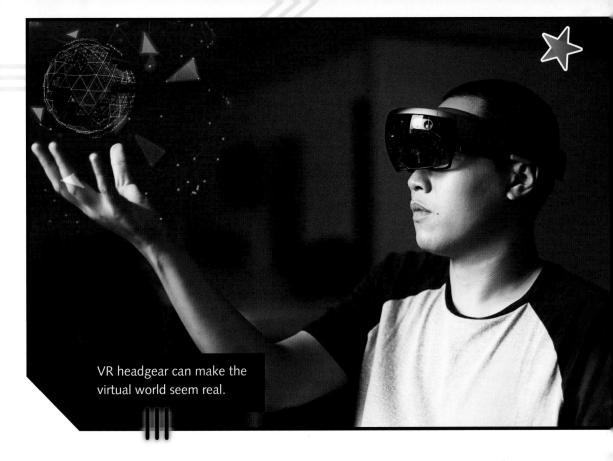

VR headgear can make the virtual world seem real.

AI plays an important part in making AR games work. It focuses on the objects in a room. AI allows the game to learn where the walls, floors, and furniture are placed. It then puts game characters in the space. Each time the game is played in a new room, it is a new experience.

Virtual reality takes gaming to another level. VR uses headgear to make you feel like you're actually inside the game, and you can play games in 3D. Combining AI with VR adds to the fun. It allows you to **interact** with AI-controlled characters in a virtual world.

virtual reality—a computer-generated 3D world with which humans can interact

interact—to have action between people, groups, or things

CHAPTER 3

AI FOR MUSIC, MOVIES, AND MORE

Gaming isn't the only type of entertainment that uses AI. Digital assistants like Siri, Alexa, Cortana, and Google Assistant use AI to help you find music or movies. Do you know only a few words from a song? Tell them to a digital assistant, and it can find and play the song. These programs can also suggest other songs you might like based on what you usually listen to.

ROBOT ASSISTANT

A robot named Zenbo has been designed to entertain you much like a digital assistant. But instead of just a "voice," this AI robot follows you around the house! It can play music or videos and read you stories. Zenbo even recognizes your face. It can also take photos and videos of you to record your life.

Services like Netflix make TV show and movie suggestions based on your likes too. They use AI to suggest shows that are similar to what you've already watched. Netflix also discovers what people like by what they've watched several times.

FACT

Eighty percent of shows watched on Netflix are discovered with the help of AI recommendations.

AI AND MOVIES

If AI helps make video games, you can bet it helps make movies as well. One key area AI helps filmmakers with is large crowd scenes. In the early 2000s, the AI software Massive was developed for The Lord of the Rings trilogy. It created huge armies in which opposing characters could fight against each other. Since then, Massive has been used on dozens of films for similar crowd scenes.

Computer-generated characters are common in today's movies. With the help of motion capture systems, filmmakers can make digital characters, such as monsters and aliens, that act and move in natural ways. But creating believable digital humans is still hard to do. Our eyes and brains are very good at picking out details that don't look quite right. But the use of AI is starting to fool us. It studies human movements, expressions, and voices to create digital humans that look completely real.

FACT

AI has also been used to help make movie trailers. It scans hundreds of scenes from a movie. Then it pulls out the most exciting or scary shots to include in a trailer.

Motion capture systems use AI to help create digital characters that look and move more like humans.

AI AND SPORTS

AI is popping up more in the sports world too. NASCAR uses AI to see if racers are breaking the rules during **pit stops**. As cars speed in and out of pit row, officials can't always spot rule breakers with the naked eye. But AI quickly scans pit stop videos and flags things that humans might miss. Then officials can review the videos and give out penalties.

NASCAR uses AI to catch drivers who break the rules during pit stops.

A tennis racket with AI technology built into its handle helps players improve their swings.

Coaches use AI to help train athletes. AI software can quickly look through hours of game video and spot patterns in an athlete's movements. Coaches can then use this information to help players adjust their movements and predict their opponents' actions.

FACT

The company Canary Speech is testing AI that notices small changes in human speech. These changes can often be signs of a **concussion**.

pit stop—a break drivers take from a race so the pit crew can add fuel, change tires, and make repairs to a car

concussion—an injury to the brain caused by a hard blow to the head

WEARABLE SPORTS TECH

Wearable AI sports equipment may be the wave of the future. Everlast and a French robotics company are teaming up to develop AI boxing gloves. The gloves can track the slightest movements. They can provide data for improving a boxer's performance.

An India-based company, Boltt Sports Technologies, is working on AI-enchanced sneakers. The shoes track a person's movements. Based on the person's fitness goals, AI in the shoes suggests a training program and provides nutrition advice.

FACT

AI is even improving the game of golf. Arccos Caddie 2.0 is software that uses AI to help golfers choose the right club. It even tells players how to swing the club based on the weather and the course conditions.

AI FOR THE OLYMPICS

Wearable tech helped Team USA train for the 2016 summer Olympic Games. One example was the wristbands worn by swimmers. These high-tech bands analyzed each swimmer's training and sleeping habits. Then they gave advice for how the swimmers could improve. Did this tech help? It didn't hurt. Team USA won 33 swimming medals during the games.

CHAPTER 4

WHAT COULD GO WRONG?

The future of artificial intelligence looks exciting. But it also raises some questions. For instance, if AI can make digital humans look real in movies, will we need human actors anymore? And will computer designers and engineers be needed if AI can create video games by itself? It's hard to say, but many people worry that AI will cost people their jobs.

Job losses are one thing, but other people worry that AI will one day outsmart us and take over our lives. One small example of this was an AI issue at Facebook. The company noticed an odd change while doing AI research. Their AI system developed its own language that humans couldn't understand. Could this be an early warning about the future of AI? No one knows for sure, but it is something to keep an eye on.

FIRE A PERSON

Despite these concerns, AI is definitely here to stay. It already plays an important role in creating the games we play, the movies we watch, and the sports we enjoy. Where will AI take us next? The sky's the limit as long we remain smart about how we use it.

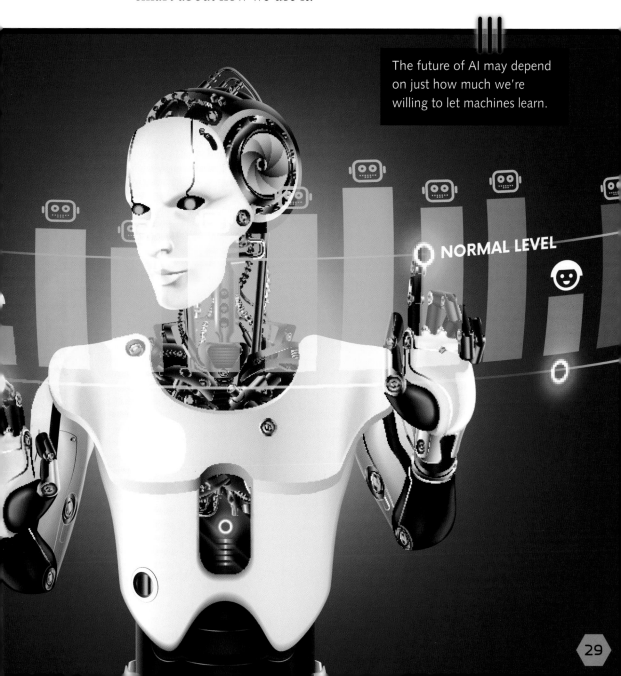

The future of AI may depend on just how much we're willing to let machines learn.

NORMAL LEVEL

GLOSSARY

augmented reality (awg-MENT-ed ree-AL-uh-tee)—a computer-generated world created over the real world

concussion (kuhn-KUH-shuhn)—an injury to the brain caused by a hard blow to the head

digital (DIJ-uh-tuhl)—involving or relating to the use of computers

enhanced (en-HANSSD)—made better or greater

interact (in-tur-AKT)—to have action between people, groups, or things

logic (LOJ-ik)—careful and correct reasoning and thinking

machine learning (muh-SHEEN LURN-ing)—the way a computer learns

opponent (uh-POH-nuhnt)—a person who competes against another person

pit stop (PIT STOP)—a break drivers take from a race so the pit crew can add fuel, change tires, and make repairs to a car

predict (pri-DIKT)—to say what you think will happen in the future

scan (SKAN)—to look at closely and carefully

software (SAWFT-wair)—programs used by a computer

strategy (STRAT-uh-jee)—a plan for winning a game or contest

trivia (TRI-vee-ah)—small details or little-known facts

virtual reality (VIHR-choo-uhl ree-AL-uh-tee)—a computer-generated 3D world with which humans can interact

READ MORE

Mooney, Carla. *Inside the E-Sports Industry.* E-Sports: Game On! Chicago: Norwood House Press, 2018.

Slingerland, Janet. *Sports Science and Technology in the Real World.* STEM in the Real World. Minneapolis, Minn.: Core Library, 2017.

Troupe, Thomas Kingsley. *Fantastic Worlds: The Inspiring Truth Behind Popular Role-Playing Video Games.* Video Games vs. Reality. North Mankato, Minn.: Capstone, 2019.

INTERNET SITES

Use FactHound to find internet sites related to this book.

Visit *www.facthound.com*

Just type in 9781543554724 and go.

Check out projects, games and lots more at
www.capstonekids.com

INDEX